YO-CXM-314

LET'S GO

SAN FRANCISCO

POCKET CITY GUIDE

Illustrations by Stephan Van Dam, VanDam Inc.
St. Martin's Press 🦋 New York

EDITOR
Sarah Robinson
RESEARCHER-WRITERS
Caitlin Casey, Heather Jackie Thomason,
Jordan Blair Woods
With thanks to Michael B. Murphy, editor of
Let's Go: San Francisco

HELPING LET'S GO: If you want to share your discoveries, suggestions, or corrections, drop us a line. Address mail to:

San Francisco Pocket City Guide
67 Mount Auburn Street
Cambridge, MA 02138 USA

Visit Let's Go at **www.letsgo.com,** or send email to:
feedback@letsgo.com
Subject: "San Francisco Pocket City Guide"

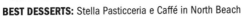

LET'S GO PICKS

BEST DESSERTS: Stella Pasticceria e Caffé in North Beach

BEST GAY CLUB: SF Badlands in the Castro

BEST STREET FOR TONING YOUR CALVES: Gough St, between Union and Sacramento.

BEST MEAL FOR UNDER $7: Kate's Kitchen in the Haight

BEST WAY TO SPEND A RAINY AFTERNOON: Picnic in the Public Art Space in SoMa

BEST PLACES TO SEE A DRAG SHOW: Marlena's in Hayes Valley and Asia SF in SoMa

BEST PLACE TO GET HOT AND SWEATY: Funky Door Yoga

BEST CLUBS FOR CRUISING: SF Badlands in the Castro and Bambuddha Lounge in the Tenderloin

BEST HANGOVER FOOD: Lori's Diner in Union Square

TOP 10 THINGS TO SEE & DO

10. CASTRO STREET ON FRIDAY AND SATURDAY NIGHTS. Before they duck into bars or head to SoMa for the clubs, San Francisco's beautiful gay boys and girls stroll Castro St. Don't come looking for a spectacle—this is high-class.

9. DIM SUM IN CHINATOWN. Sample delectable Chinese brunch delights—everything from traditional shrimp dumplings to chicken feet (mmm, crunchy!). Just about any restaurant in Chinatown will do.

8. THE EXPLORATORIUM. Hands-on science at this museum will captivate both kids and kids-at-heart. The huge space is crammed with contraptions to climb through and play with.

7. ALCATRAZ. The Rock is the coolest attraction in the Bay. The original high security civilian prison, this popular tourist destination offers excellent guided tours that tell its many stories in chilling detail.

6. THE SAN FRANCISCO ART INSTITUTE. Diego Rivera, just one of the many artistic hot shots to have studied and taught at this gorgeous hilltop hideaway, left his mark in 1931 with a fresco depicting the city.

5. MUIR WOODS. Experience the mysterious, magical stillness of the centuries-old redwoods that loom above you in silence. George Lucas was so impressed that he filmed *Return of the Jedi* here.

4. GOLDEN GATE PARK. GG Park is the largest urban park in the United States. (Central what?) You could spend a day or five seeing the sights and the bison in this lush paradise.

3. MISSION MURALS. This urban art deftly combines artistic excellence and community politics. Standouts include Balmy Alley and a three-building tribute to guitar god Carlos Santana.

2. A GIANTS GAME AT PAC BELL PARK. Bleacher seats to a Giants game come with fabulous views of the game, the city, and the Bay. You could see a right-field homer make a splash.

1. GOLDEN GATE BRIDGE. You can see the bridge from all over the city (and on two out of every three postcards), but to truly know its immense beauty, you gotta be there.

BEST OF SAN FRANCISCO

FISHERMAN'S WHARF & THE PIERS

Fisherman's Wharf is home to eight blocks of touristy carnival-esque aquatic splendor. Cheesy t-shirt shops and garish storefronts share the area with some fun museums. **Piers 39 through 45** house some of San Francisco's most iconic attractions. **Ghirardelli Square,** the **Cannery,** and the western edge of the wharf are calmer than Pier 39, with their stunning Bay views, sultry courtyard jazz, and tasty eateries.

MARINA, FT. MASON, & COW HOLLOW

The residential Marina is home to more young, wealthy professionals than any other part of San Francisco. Neighboring Fort Mason contains a number of theaters and museums. Directly across the Marina Green stand the breathtaking **Palace of Fine Arts** and the **Exploratorium.** A few blocks south, Cow Hollow houses herds of the city's elite. Here, cafes, boutiques, and galleries buzz by day, but by dinnertime the bars are swarming with yuppie singles on the prowl.

NORTH BEACH

North Beach, a primarily Italian community and the birthplace of the **Beat movement,** lies north of Chinatown. In the early 1950s, a group of writers including Jack Kerouac, Allen Ginsberg, and Lawrence Ferlinghetti came to here to write, drink, and raise some hell. Today, though, North Beach attracts a crowd of finely-clad city-dwellers who flock to its Italian restaurants and stay for the cozy bar scene and hot live acts.

UNION SQUARE

Union's big scene is retail. It is home to chic shops, ritzy hotels, and prestigious art galleries. It's also the heart of San Francisco's theater district.

CHINATOWN

The largest Chinese community outside of Asia, Chinatown is also the most densely populated of San Francisco's neighborhoods. Today, the area attracts visitors with its abundance of affordable eateries and markets.

NOB HILL & RUSSIAN HILL

In the late 19th century, Nob Hill attracted the West's great railroad magnates and robber barons. Their mansions still sparkle today. Russian Hill, equally gawk-worthy, is also largely residential.

GOLDEN GATE BRIDGE & THE PRESIDIO

The Golden Gate Bridge reaches across the San Francisco Bay from Marin County to the Presidio. Origi-

NEIGHBORHOODS

nally a military garrison, the Presidio is wide open to the public. Its miles of paths and hills, especially Crissy Field, are worth a visit.

SOUTH OF MARKET AREA (SOMA)

The most visited, culturally rich part of SoMa lies north of Folsom St, between 2nd and 4th St. These blocks are filled with the concrete and glass expanses of Yerba Buena Gardens, Sony Metreon, and the Moscone Convention Center, as well as the **San Francisco Museum of Modern Art (SFMoMA).**

HAIGHT-ASHBURY

The Haight has aged with uneven grace since its hippie heyday. "Hashbury" embraced drug use and Eastern philosophies during anti-Vietnam War protests and marches, and. reached its apogee in 1967's "Summer of Love." Today the counterculture hangs out with the over-the-counter tourist culture.

CASTRO

This is where the boys are. Much of San Francisco's **gay community** (mostly male along with a smaller number of young lesbians) makes the Castro home. Cruisy bars and cafes are everywhere, same-sex public displays of affection raise nary an eyebrow, and tank tops and chiseled abs are *de rigueur*. Aside from being fabulous, the Castro is also pretty.

MISSION

Founded by Spanish settlers in 1776, the Mission is home to some of the city's oldest structures. A prominent **Latino** presence has long defined the Mission. Politically, this up-and-coming district is the city's most radical pocket, marked by left-wing bookstores, active labor associations, and bohemian bars. The area is also home to a cohesive lesbian community.

TENDERLOIN

Sporadic attempts at urban renewal have done a bit to improve the poverty of Tenderloin, and its nightlife scene is getting hot. Nevertheless, *avoid walking here alone*, especially in the rectangle bordered by Ellis St, Van Ness Av, Leavenworth St, and Golden Gate Av.

LINCOLN PARK

Lincoln Park's great chunk of green is positioned perfectly for snapping a shot of the Golden Gate Bridge and the Bay. Rugged terrain for hiking and biking meets high culture at the **California Palace of the Legion of Honor.**

NEIGHBORHOODS

GOLDEN GATE PARK

Beginning in the 1870s, the city undertook a decades-long project to transform a desert-like region into a vibrant green patch of loveliness. Today, nine lakes, a herd of bison, two windmills, and a science center can be found on the 1017 lush acres of the park.

FINANCIAL DISTRICT & EMBARCADERO

Corporate worker bees swarm the Financial District, where towering banks blot out the cheerful sun. A surprising number of parks and architectural stand-outs add character to the area.

CIVIC CENTER AND HAYES VALLEY

There's no mistaking the colossal Civic Center, with its mammoth classical buildings arranged around two vast plazas. Home to the opera, symphony, and most of San Francisco's major theater, the district is grandest at night. Nearby Hayes Valley is small and increasingly upscale since a drastic makeover refurbished it after the 1989 earthquake.

PACIFIC HEIGHTS & JAPANTOWN

Stunning views of the city and the Bay, the legendary **Fillmore Street jazz scene,** and elegantly restored Victorian homes put Pacific Heights on the map. Japantown, down Fillmore St, for a time constituted one of the largest Japanese enclaves outside Japan.

RICHMOND

This mainly residential area is home to Irish-, Russian-, and Chinese-Americans. East of Park Presidio Blvd., the Inner Richmond is festooned with cut-price grocery stores and excellent ethnic cuisine.

ALCATRAZ & ANGEL ISLAND

It once housed the nation's most hardened criminals, but today Alcatraz draws boatloads of tourists each day. Angel Island was used in the late 19th century as a detention center for Chinese immigrants and later as a WWII POW camp. Today, its shores and trails are surprisingly perfect for picnicking and hiking.

SUNSET

It may look like a flat, suburban sprawl on the map, but the Sunset has a lot to offer. This middle-class and student-heavy district is an untarnished slice of "real life." For the visitor, fantastic cheap food, used bookstores, lively cafes, and laid-back bars makes the 15min. MUNI ride from Haight-Ashbury worthwhile.

NEIGHBORHOODS

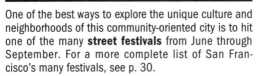
One of the best ways to explore the unique culture and neighborhoods of this community-oriented city is to hit one of the many **street festivals** from June through September. For a more complete list of San Francisco's many festivals, see p. 30.

Haight Street Fair: The Summer of Love may have ended, but Haight Street still sports colorful characters and lots of tie-dye. Two stages boast musical acts from rock to reggae to blues. *(Haight St between Masonic and Stanyan. 2nd weekend in June.)*

North Beach Festival: Come to San Francisco's Little Italy for the oldest urban street fair in the country, where Italian scents meet the birthplace of beat poetry. Enjoy swing dancing in the park, spoken word performances in the street, or cappuccino outside one of the many fabulous Italian restaurants. *(North Beach. 3rd weekend in June.)*

Ghirardelli Sq. Chocolate Festival: Overload your senses with chocolate candy, ice cream, baked goods, and of course, the Ghirardelli Chocolate Store. Enter the "Earthquake" ice-cream eating contest; winner wins his weight in Ghirardelli chocolate. *(Ghirardelli Sq. 1st weekend in Sept.)*

Folsom Street Fair: Leave shyness behind as you join San Francisco's more sexually liberated folk as they show off their leather, bondage gear, whips, and chains. So polish your piercings, put a leash on your travel buddy, and ogle the kinkiest crowd you'll ever see parading in public. *(Folsom St between 7th and 12th St. 4th weekend in Sept.)*

BEST WAYS TO TURN HEADS IN SF

7. Opt to keep your shirt *on* at an unforgettable (and unforgettably late) Friday at **The EndUp** in SoMa.

6. Show up fully clothed to the **Folson Street Fair** (see above).

5. Be a little "too old" to play in the Tactile Dome at the **Exploratorium.**

4. Offend this liberal city's sensibilities by ordering a burger at the award-winning **Millennium** restaurant.

3. Show off your knowledge of Beatnik literary culture at **City Lights Bookstore** in North Beach.

2. Escape the crowds with your drink and climb the ladder to "jail" at **Odeon Bar** in the Mission.

1. Look fabulous and strut your stuff down **Castro Street** on a weekend evening.

HIGHLIGHTS SIGHTS

FISHERMAN'S WHARF & THE PIERS

PIER 39 (#13, A14). Self-titled "San Francisco's Number One Attraction," Pier 39 is a shamelessly commercial collection of 110 speciality shops, restaurants, vendors, and entertainment. For a whirlwind city-tour, experience **The Great San Francisco Adventure** at **Pier 39 Cinemax.** In huge-screen format, you can fly over the Golden Gate Bridge, feel a 3.0 scale earthquake, race down Lombard St, watch a 49ers game, and dive to the ocean depths. If that leaves you feeling giddy, head to the end of the pier to unwind with live street performances at **Center Stage** or a jaunt on the **Venetian Carousel.** (☎ 981-7437. Shops, attractions, and fast food open Su-Th 10am-9pm, F-Sa 10am-10pm; restaurants open Su-Th 11:30am-10pm, F-Sa 11:30am-11pm. Cinemax: ☎ 956-3456. Shows every 45min. First show 10am. Adults $7.50, seniors $6, children $4.50. California Welcome Center and Internet Cafe: ☎ 956-3493. Open Su-Th 9am-9pm, F-Sa 9am-10pm.)

PIER 45 (A9, A13-A14). Still used by fishermen in the early morning, Pier 45 is also home to the **USS Pampanito** (SS-383). In retirement after sinking six enemy ships during its Pacific patrols, this WWII *Balao*-class fleet submarine is now a National Historic Park museum. (☎ 775-1943. Open June-Sept. M-Th 9am-6pm, F-Su 9am-8pm; Oct.-May M-Tu and Th-Su 9am-8pm, W 9am-6pm. Adults $7, seniors $5, ages 6-12 $4, under 6 free.)

GHIRARDELLI SQUARE (#24, A13). Chocolate-lovers' heaven, Ghirardelli Square, houses a mall in what used to be a chocolate factory. Both the **Ghirardelli Chocolate Manufactory,** with its vast selection of chocolatey goodies, and the **Ghirardelli Chocolate Shop and Caffe,** with drinks, frozen yogurt, and a smaller selection of chocolates, hand out free samples of chocolate at the door—we know that's why you came. The **soda fountain,** an old-fashioned ice-cream parlor, serves huge sundaes ($6.25) smothered with its world-famous hot fudge sauce. (Mall: 900 North Point St. ☎ 775-5500. Stores open M-Sa 10am-9pm, Su 10am-6pm. Ghirardelli Chocolate Manufactory: ☎ 771-4903. Open Su-Th 10am-11pm, F-Sa 10am-midnight. Soda fountain open Su-Th 10am-11pm, F-Sa 10am-midnight. Chocolate Shop and Caffe: ☎ 474-1414. Open M-Th 8:30am-9pm, F 8:30am-10pm, Sa 9am-10pm, Su 9am-9pm.)

HYDE STREET PIER (A9, A13). Along with the curving Municipal Pier, Hyde Street Pier encloses an area of the Bay known as the Aquatic Park. Sittin' on the dock of the Bay, you can watch the daring locals swim laps in frigid 50°F water. If you feel like joining in, the **South End Rowing Club** and the **Dolphin Club** are open to the public on alternate days for $6.50. Hyde Street Pier is also part of the National Historic Park, offering guided tours of the vessels, schooners, and ferryboats as well as a boat-building class to satisfy your nautical needs. *(On Hyde St. ☎561-7100. Open 9:30am-5:30pm. Adults $5, under 16 free. Guided Pier Walks offered 4 times daily; call for times. Dolphin Club: 502 Jefferson St. ☎441-9329. Open in summer W 11am-6pm; in winter 10am-5pm. South End Rowing Club: 500 Jefferson St. ☎929-9656. Open in summer Tu, Th, and Sa 11am-6pm; in winter 10am-5pm. Boating Class: ☎929-0202.)*

THE CANNERY (#22, A13). Built in 1907 as the del Monte canning factory and once the largest peach cannery in the world, **The Cannery** has been converted into a marketplace-style plaza with a maze of shady terraces and European-inspired garden courtyards. Three levels of balconies, bridges, and walkways house some charming restaurants and shops. *(2801 Leavenworth St. www.thecannery.com.)*

MARINA

PALACE OF FINE ARTS (#26, A11). With its open-air domed structure and curving colonnades, the **Palace of Fine Arts** is one of the best picnic spots in the city. Shakespearean plays are often performed here during the summer. *(On Baker St., between Jefferson and Bay St next to the Exploratorium. Open daily 6am-9pm. Free.)* The **Palace of Fine Arts Theater,** located directly behind the rotunda, also hosts various dance and theater performances and film festivals. *(☎563-6504; www.palaceoffinearts.com. Call for shows, times, and ticket prices.)*

EXPLORATORIUM (#26, A11). The Exploratorium can hold over 4000 people, and when admission is free, it usually does. Over 650 interactive displays—including miniature tornadoes, computer planet-managing, and giant bubble-makers—explain the wonders of the world. The Tactile Dome—a dark maze of tunnels, slides, nooks, and crannies—refines your sense of touch. *(3601 Lyon St. ☎563-7337. Open June-Aug. daily 10am-6pm; Sept.-May Tu-Su 10am-5pm. $12; students, seniors, disabled, and ages 9-17 $9.50; ages 4-8 $8, under 3 free. Free first W of each month. Tactile Dome $15, reservations recommended.)*

WAVE ORGAN (#17, A12). Past the Golden Gate Yacht Club at the end of a long jetty rests one of San Francisco's best hidden treasures: the Wave Organ, an acoustic environmental sculpture made up of 25 pipes jutting out of the ocean that create musical sounds as waves crash against it. Conceived by Peter Richards, the project was completed in 1986. George Gonzalez, a sculptor and stonemason, designed the seating area around the pipes using granite and marble pieces from a decimated cemetery. All sorts of carvings can be discerned if you look closely. The music itself is quite subtle, like listening to a sea shell, and is best heard at high tide.

NORTH BEACH

WASHINGTON SQUARE (#31, B14). Washington Sq, bordered by Union, Filbert, Stockton, and Powell St, is North Beach's *piazza*, a pretty, not-quite-square, tree-lined lawn. The statue in Washington Sq is of Benjamin Franklin. The wedding site of Marilyn Monroe and Joe DiMaggio, the park fills every morning with practitioners of *tai chi*. By noon, sunbathers, picnickers, and bocce-ball players take over. At 666 Filbert St, the **St. Peter and St. Paul Catholic Church** beckons tired sightseers to take refuge in its dark, wooden nave.

TELEGRAPH HILL (A9, A15). Overlooking Washington Park and North Beach, Telegraph Hill was originally the site of a semaphore that signaled the arrival of ships in Gold Rush days. Today, tourists hike up the hill to visit **Coit Tower,** which stands 210 ft. high and commands a spectacular view of the city and the Bay. During the Depression, the government's Works Progress Administration employed artists to paint the murals on the dome's inside. *(MUNI bus #39 goes all the way to Coit Tower. If driving, follow Lombard St to the top, where there is free 30min. parking M and F 9am-5pm, Tu-Th and Sa-Su 8am-5pm. Tower: ☎ 362-0808. Open daily 10am-7pm. **Elevator fare:** Adults $3.75, over 64 $2.50, ages 6-12 $1.50, under 6 free. Free guided tours of murals Th 10:15am, Sa 11am.)*

CITY LIGHTS BOOKSTORE (#36, B14-15). Drawn by low rents and cheap bars, the Beat writers came to national attention when Lawrence Ferlinghetti's City Lights Bookstore, opened in 1953, published Allen Ginsberg's Howl. City Lights now stocks a wide selection of fiction and poetry. Black and white signs beckon visitors to sit down, turn off their "sell-phones," and flip through the books. *(2261 Columbus Av. ☎ 362-8193. Open daily 10am-midnight.)*

CHINATOWN

WAVERLY PLACE (#44, B14). Find this little alley (between Sacramento and Washington St. and between Stockton St and Grant Av) and you'll want to spend all day gazing at the incredible architecture. The fire escapes are painted in pinks and greens

8

and held together by railings made of intricate Chinese patterns. Tourists can also visit **Tien Hou Temple,** 125 Waverly Pl, the oldest Chinese temple in the US.

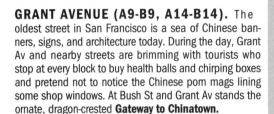

GRANT AVENUE (A9-B9, A14-B14). The oldest street in San Francisco is a sea of Chinese banners, signs, and architecture today. During the day, Grant Av and nearby streets are brimming with tourists who stop at every block to buy health balls and chirping boxes and pretend not to notice the Chinese porn mags lining some shop windows. At Bush St and Grant Av stands the ornate, dragon-crested **Gateway to Chinatown.**

ROSS ALLEY (#37, B14). Ross Alley was once lined with brothels and gambling houses; today, it has the cramped look of old Chinatown. The narrow street has stood in for the Orient in such films as *Big Trouble in Little China, Karate Kid II,* and *Indiana Jones and the Temple of Doom.* Squeeze into a tiny doorway to watch fortune cookies being shaped by hand at the **Golden Gate Cookie Company.** *(56 Ross Alley. ☎ 781-3956. Bag of cookies $3, with "funny," "sexy," or "lucky" fortunes $5. Open daily 10am-8pm.)*

NOB HILL & RUSSIAN HILL

THE CROOKEDEST STREET IN THE WORLD (#28, A13). The famous curves of **Lombard Street** seem to grace half of San Francisco's postcards, and rightfully so. The flowerbeds along the curves are beautifully manicured and the eight curves themselves—installed in the 1920s so that horse-drawn carriages could negotiate the extremely steep hill—are uniquely San Francisco. From the top of Lombard St, pedestrians and passengers alike enjoy a fantastic view of the city and harbor. *(Between Hyde and Leavenworth St, running down Russian Hill.)*

GRACE CATHEDRAL & HUNTINGTON PARK (#46, B14). The largest Gothic edifice west of the Mississippi, **Grace Cathedral** is Nob Hill's stained-glass-studded crown. The main doors are replicas cast from Lorenzo Ghiberti's *Doors on Paradise* in Florence's Duomo Cathedral. Inside, the altar of the AIDS Interfaith Memorial Chapel celebrates the church's "inclusive community of love" with a Keith Haring triptych. *(1100 California St, between Jones and Taylor St. ☎ 749-6300; www.gracecathedral.org. Open Su-F 7am-6pm, Sa 8am-6pm. Services: Su 7:30, 8:15, 11am, 3, and 6pm; M-F 7:30, 9am, 12:10, and 5:15pm; Sa 9, 11am, and 3pm. Tour guides available M-F 1-3pm, Sa 11:30am-1:30pm, Su 1:30-2pm. Suggested donation $3.)*

UNION SQUARE

MAIDEN LANE (#51, C14). When the Financial District was down and dirty, Union Square's Morton Alley was dirtier. Around 1900, murders on the Alley averaged one per week and prostitutes waved to their favorite customers from windows. After the 1906 earthquake and fires destroyed most of the brothels and tenements, merchants moved in and renamed the area Maiden Lane in hopes of transforming the street's image. Today, the pedestrian street is a pleasant place to stroll in your newly purchased Gucci shades.

FRANK LLOYD WRIGHT BUILDING (#51, C14). Maiden Lane's main architectural attraction is the Frank Lloyd Wright Building, the city's only Wright-designed structure. It was built in 1948 out of unreinforced masonry, complete with original wood cabinetry and some gravity-defying pneumatic tubes. The space now houses the Xanadu Gallery, which displays an eclectic collection of African tribal art, Han Dynasty vases, Pacific Rim sculptures, and Pre-Colombian pottery. *(140 Maiden La. Xanadu Gallery: ☎392-9999; fax 984-5856. Open M-Sa 10am-6pm.)*

GOLDEN GATE BRIDGE & THE PRESIDIO

GOLDEN GATE BRIDGE (#10, B1). Built in 1937 for only $35 million, the Golden Gate stretches across 1¼ mi. of ocean, its towers looming 65 stories above the Bay. It can sway up to 27 ft. in each direction during high winds. The views from the bridge are amazing, especially from the Vista Point in Marin County just after the bridge.

PRESIDIO (A11). When Spanish settlers forged their way up the San Francisco peninsula from Baja California in 1769, they established *presidios*, or military outposts, along the way. San Francisco's Presidio, the northernmost point of Spanish territory in North America, was dedicated in 1776. The settlement stayed in Spanish hands for only 45 years—it was passed to Mexico when the country won its independence from Spain. In 1848, the United States took over the Presidio. The **San Francisco National Cemetery** houses the graves of over 30,000 soldiers and their families and was the first national cemetery on the West Coast. *(Just off of Lincoln Blvd in the center of the Presidio. ☎650-589-7737.)*

LINCOLN PARK

CLIFF HOUSE (#54, B5). The Golden Gate National Recreation Area Visitors Center, housed within the Cliff House, distributes information on Lincoln Park, Ocean Beach, and the entire GGNRA. Don't

SIGHTS

feed the coin-operated binoculars that look out over Seal Rocks—instead, head inside for a free look through the GGNRA telescope. (☎556-8642. Open daily 10am-5pm.) Next to the Musée Mécanique, overlooking the cliffs and the Pacific, rests the **Camera Obscura**, which shows the ocean vistas and nearby Seal Rocks at 700% magnification. (☎750-0415. Open daily 11am-sunset, weather permitting. $2. Closed for renovations until summer 2004.)

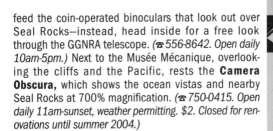

SUTRO BATHS & SUTRO HEIGHTS PARK (#63, B5).
Adolph Sutro's 1896 bathhouse, known as the Sutro Baths, lies in ruins just north of Cliff House. Up the hill from the intersection of Point Lobos and 48th Av, and to the east of the Cliff House and the Baths, is spectacular Sutro Heights Park. The park offers unparalleled views of the city and surrounding watery expanses.

PALACE OF THE LEGION OF HONOR (#55, B6).
In the middle of Lincoln Park, between the golf course and the **Land's End** wilderness, sits the magnificent California Palace of the Legion of Honor, built in 1924. A copy of Rodin's *Thinker* beckons visitors into the grand courtyard, where a little glass pyramid recalls the Louvre. A thorough catalogue of great masters, from Rubens to Dalí, hangs inside. Free tours given on Sa in a different language (either French, Spanish, or Italian) each week. Just outside the Palace, a **Holocaust Memorial** depicts the Holocaust as a mass of emaciated victims with a single survivor looking out through a barbed-wire fence to the Pacific. (☎863-3330; www.legionofhonor.org. Open Su and Tu-Sa 9:30am-5pm. Adults $8, seniors $6, under 17 $5, under 12 free. $2 discount with MUNI transfer; Tu free. Wheelchair-accessible. Memorial free.)

GOLDEN GATE PARK (#87, B5-C7)

GARDENS & SIGHTS. Despite its sandy past, the soil of Golden Gate Park is rich enough today to support a wealth of flowers, particularly in spring and summer. The magnificent **Conservatory of Flowers** is scheduled to reopen after renovations in summer 2003. On the eastern side, near the Strybing Store and Russel Library of Horticulture, is the **Garden of Fragrance,** designed for the visually impaired—all labels are in Braille and the plants are chosen specifically for their textures and scents. The **Shakespeare Garden,** filled with crab-apples and red brick, contains almost every flower and plant ever mentioned by the Bard. (Open daily dawn-dusk; in winter Su and Tu-Sa dawn-dusk. Free.) Ring-like Stow Lake sits in the middle of the park. Cross one of two stone bridges and wreak fruit-filled havoc on the big, green island of **Strawberry Hill.**

SIGHTS

The oldest Japanese garden in the US, the **Japanese Tea Garden** is a collection of wooden buildings, small pools, graceful footbridges, and carefully pruned trees. (☎ 752-4227. *Open in summer daily 8:30am-6pm; in winter 8:30am-5pm. Adults $3.50, seniors and ages 6-12 $1.25. Free for all in summer 8:30-9:30am and 5-6pm and in winter 8:30-9:30am and 4-5pm.*)

SPRECKELS LAKE & AROUND. Brimming Spreckels Lake, on JFK Dr, is populated by crowds of turtles that pile onto a big rock to sun themselves. A dozen shaggy bison loll about a spacious paddock just west of Spreckels. The Queen Wilhelmina Tulip Garden bursts forth color from 10,000 bulbs in March. Rounding out the days of yore is the Children's Playground with its carousel (circa 1912), accompanied by a $50,000 Gebruder band organ. (*Open June-Sept. daily 10am-5pm; Oct.-May Tu-W and F-Su 9am-4pm. Adults $1, ages 6-12 25¢.*)

CALIFORNIA ACADEMY OF SCIENCES (#83, B7-C7). The Academy of Sciences, east of Stow Lake, near 9th Av, houses several museums. **The Steinhart Aquarium** is home to over 600 aquatic species. The **Morrison Planetarium** holds impressive sky shows. (*Sky shows M-F 2pm, with additional summer showings. Adults $2.50; students, seniors, and ages 6-17 $1.25.*) The rest of the Academy is considered the **Natural History Museum.** Inside, the Earthquake Room explains the science of quakes famous around the Bay Area. (☎ 750-7145; www.calacademy.org. *Open June-Aug. daily 9am-6pm; Sept.-May 10am-5pm. Adults $8.50; students, seniors, and ages 12-17 $5.50; ages 4-11 $2. Extended hours and free entrance 1st W of each month. $2.50 discount for bicycle riders; indoor bike parking available. Discounts available with MUNI pass or transfer.*)

FINANCIAL DISTRICT

TRANSAMERICA PYRAMID (#42, B15). The leading lady of the city's skyline, this distinctive office building was designed to allow as much light as possible to shine on the streets below. Tight security means no chance of a top-floor view. Now a pillar of commerce, the location was once a site of revolutionary disgruntlement; Sun Yat-Sen scripted a dynastic overthrow in one of its second-floor offices. (*600 Montgomery St, between Clay and Washington St.*)

JUSTIN HERMAN PLAZA (#39, B15). When not overrun by skateboarders, the Plaza is home to bands and rallyists. U2 rock star Bono was arrested here after a concert in 1987 for spray painting "Stop the Traffic—Rock and Roll" on the fountain. Recently, the plaza has been the starting point for Critical Mass, a pro-bicyclist ride that takes place after 5pm on the last Friday of every month.

JAPANTOWN & PACIFIC HEIGHTS

SAINT DOMINIC'S ROMAN CATHOLIC CHURCH (B8, C12).

With its imposing gray stone and gothic feel, St. Dominic's is a must-see, especially for its renowned shrine of **Saint Jude,** skirted by candles and intricately carved oak. *(2390 Bush St, at Steiner St. Open M-Sa 6:30am-5:30pm, Su 7:30am-9pm. Mass M-F 6:30, 8am, 5:30pm, Sa 8am, 5:30pm, Su 7:30, 9:30, 11:30am, 1:30, 5:30, 9pm candlelight service.)*

SOUTH OF MARKET AREA (SOMA)

SAN FRANCISCO MUSEUM OF MODERN ART (SFMOMA) (#57, C15).

This marble-trimmed museum houses five spacious floors of art, with emphasis on design, photography, and audiovisuals. SFMoMA has the most 20th-century art this side of New York, including collections of Warhol, Johns, Rauschenberg, and Stella. *(151 3rd St, between Mission and Howard St. ☎ 357-4000; www.sfmoma.org. Open Sept. 3-May 24 M-Tu and F-Su 11am-5:45pm, Th 11am-8:45pm; May 25-Sept. 2 M-Tu and F-Su 10am-6pm, Th 10am-9pm. Adults $10, over 62 $7, students with valid ID $6, under 13 free. Th 6-9pm half-price. Free 1st Tu of each month. Four free tours per day.)*

YERBA BUENA CENTER FOR THE ARTS (#62, C15).

The center runs an excellent theater and gallery space that emphasizes performance, film, viewer involvement, and local multicultural work—essentially anything that can be considered "adventurous art." It is surrounded by the **Yerba Buena Rooftop Gardens.** *(701 Mission St, at 3rd St. ☎ 978-2787; www.yerbabuenaarts.org. Open Su and Tu-Sa 11am-6pm. Adults $6, free 1st Tu of month; seniors and students $3, free every Th. Free tours Th 5pm and Sa 4pm.)*

ZEUM (#66, C15).

Within the gardens but a sight unto itself, this completely interactive "art and technology center" is aimed primarily at children and teens. Beside studios for arts and crafts, claymation, and karaoke, Zeum has a music performance space, an ice skating rink, a bowling center, and a carousel that was built in 1906. *(221 4th St, at Howard St. ☎ 777-2800; www.zeum.org. Open in summer Tu-Su 11am-5pm, off-season W-Su 11am-5pm. Adults $7, students and seniors $6, ages 4-18 $5, under 4 free. Carousel: open daily 11am-6pm. $2 for 2 rides.)*

MISSION

MISSION DOLORES (#90, C9).
Founded in 1776 in the old heart of San Francisco, the Mission Dolores is thought to be the city's oldest building. *(3321 16th St, at Dolores St. ☎621-8203. Open May-Oct. daily 9am-4:30pm; Nov.-Apr. 9am-4pm. Adults $3, ages 5-12 $2. Mass: in English M-F 7:30, 9am; Sa 7:30, 9am, 5pm; Su 8, 10am. In Spanish Su noon.)*

MISSION MURALS (C9).
The Mission's magnificent murals are located along 24th St. Continuing the tradition made famous by Diego Rivera and Jose Orozco, the murals have been a source of pride for Chicanos in the area since the 1980s.

ALCATRAZ (#7, B2)

In its 29 years as a maximum-security federal penitentiary, Alcatraz encountered a menacing cast of characters: Al "Scarface" Capone, George "Machine Gun" Kelly, and Robert "The Birdman" Stroud, among others. There were 14 escape attempts—some desperate, defiant bolts for freedom, others carefully calculated and innovative. On the Rock, the award-winning cellhouse audio tour takes you back to the infamous days of Alcatraz. *(The Blue and Gold Fleet (☎705-8200, tickets 705-5555) runs to Alcatraz (14 per day; $9.25 round-trip, seniors $7.50, ages 5-11 $6; audio tour $4 extra). Reserve at least a day and preferably a week in advance, especially in summer.)*

ANGEL ISLAND (A2)

Picturesque **Angel Island State Park** sits in the middle of San Francisco Bay. A 20min. ferry ride from San Francisco or Marin brings you to rolling hills, biking and hiking trails, and sprawling picnic grounds. The forts left here by the US Army have housed a Civil War encampment, a Spanish-American War quarantine station, a missile site, and an immigration station. From 1910 to 1940, the island served as a holding site for immigrants, mostly Chinese. During WWII, the station was a POW camp. Today, the island is a heavenly escape from the city, except for those sunny weekends when all of San Francisco shows up. The **Park Ranger Station** holds tours including the Immigration Station, Camp Reynolds, and Fort McDowell. *(Camp Info: reservations ☎800-444-7275; www.park-net.com. 7-night max. stay. Max. 8 people per campsite. Check-in 2pm. Check-out noon. $7 per night. Visitor Center, ☎435-3522. Open Apr.–Oct. 10am-5pm. Bike Rental, near the docks at Ayala Cove. $10 per hr.; $30 per day. Tandems $15 per hr.; $50 per day. Child trailers $5 per hr.; $15 per day. Helmets free with rental. Open M-F 10am-3pm, Sa-Su 10am-4pm. MC/V.)*

SIGHTS

EATING IN SAN FRANCISCO

RESTAURANT	AREA	PAGE	MAP
AMERICAN			
Cafe Bosse	SoMa	16	D13
Dottie's True Blue Café	Union Square	16	C14
Equinox	Financial Dist.	20	B15
Home	Castro	18	C9
Pat's Café	Fisherman's	17	A14
Perry's	Cow Hollow	21	B12
The Stinking Rose	North Beach	21	B14
ASIAN FUSION			
Ponzu	Union Square	19	C14
Welcome Home	Castro	17	C18
BREAKFAST			
Kate's Kitchen	Lower Haight	16	D12
Pat's Café	Fisherman's	17	A14
CAFES			
Café Bean	Union Square	16	C14
Squat and Gobble	Upper Haight	19	D11
CALIFORNIAN			
Cafe Venue	Financial Dist.	18	C14
Cal. Culinary Academy	Tenderloin	20	C13
foreign cinema	Mission	20	C9
Zuni	Hayes Valley	21	D13
CHINESE			
House of Nanking	Chinatown	16	B14
Lee Hou	Richmond	19	B7
DESSERT			
Bombay Ice Creamery	Mission	16	C9
Golden Gate Bakery	Chinatown	16	B14
Stella Pasticceria e Caffè	North Beach	17	B14
FRENCH			
The Butler and the Chef	SoMa	16	C15
INDIAN			
Mela Tandoori	Union Square	17	C14
ITALIAN			
Aperto	Potrero Hill	20	C10
Pane e Vino	Marina	21	B12
Steps of Rome	North Beach	19	B14
JAPANESE			
Isobune	Japantown	16	C12
Juban	Japantown	18	C12
Umeko	Japantown	21	C13
MEDITERRANEAN			
La Méditerranée	Pacific Heights	17	C12
PIZZA			
Café Abo	Mission	18	D9
Marcello's	Castro	17	C8
Pizza Inferno	Pacific Heights	17	C12
Pizza Orgasmica	Cow Hollow	19	B12
SEAFOOD			
McCormick and Kuleto's	Fisherman's	20	A13
SPANISH			
Charanga	Mission	18	C9
THAI			
Laltai Thai	Civic Center	19	C14
Nirvana	Castro	17	C8
VEGETARIAN			
Ananda Fuara	Civic Center	18	D13
Café Abo	Mission	18	D9
Cafe Bosse	SoMa	16	D13
Greens	Fort Mason	20	A13
Nirvana	Castro	17	C8
Millennium	Civic Center	21	C14
VIETNAMESE			
The Golden Turtle	Russian Hill	18	B13

RESTAURANTS BY TYPE FOOD

15

Bombay Ice Creamery
548 Valencia St

It's not just the ice cream, but also the food that merits a visit to Bombay. The mango *kulfi* ($2.50) is to die for (get it with rose water and sweet rice noodles). The *bhel* (a puffed rice dish; $3.50) and the *dhai puris* ($3.50) are both delicious. Open Tu-Su 11am-8pm. **C9**

The Butler and the Chef
155A South Park Av

Pierre serves breakfast crepes ($3-7), delicious *croque-monsieur* or baguette sandwiches (from $6), and a huge assortment of wine ($4) in a stellar reproduction of a Parisian street cafe. Open M 7:30am-6pm, Tu-Sa 7:30am-9:30pm. **C15**

Café Bean
800 Sutter St

All-day breakfasts like steaming eggs and toast ($4) and Dutch pancakes ($4) or hearty lunch fare like huge barbecue turkey sandwiches ($6.50) make Café Bean attractive to tourists, business people, and wayward hipsters. Open M-Sa 6am-7pm, Su 6am-5pm. **C14**

Cafe Bosse
1599 Howard St

Bosse serves restaurant-quality meals in a cafeteria-style decor. Burgers, breakfast omelettes, and lunch specials (all $6-7). Try the Philly cheesesteak. Lots of veggie and salad options, too. Open M-F 7am-4pm. **D13**

Dottie's True Blue Café
522 Jones St

Hearty portions and quirky variations like chicken-apple sausage and the grilled eggplant with goat-cheese sandwich ($6) often keep a line waiting outside. Open M and Th-Su 7:30am-3pm. **C14**

Golden Gate Bakery
1029 Grant Av

This tiny bakery's moon cakes, noodle puffs, and vanilla cream buns (all $.75-1.50) draw long lines of tourists and locals. Open daily 8am-8pm. No credit cards. **B14**

House of Nanking
919 Kearny St

Big, high-quality portions offset a low-key setting and a low-key check in this famous Chinatown institution. Many entrees under $8. Open M-F 11am-10pm, Sa noon-10pm, Su noon-9:30pm. **B14**

Isobune
1737 Post St

In the Kintetsu Bldg., upper level. Swipe sushi as it sails by your moat-side seat in America's first sushi boat restaurant. Color-coded plates correspond to prices ($1.50-3.75). Sake $3. Open daily 11:30am-10pm. **C12**

Kate's Kitchen
471 Haight St

One of the best breakfasts in the neighborhood, served all day. Try the "French Toast Orgy," with fruit, yogurt, and granola ($5.25). Open M 9am-2:45pm, Tu-F 8am-2:45pm, Sa-Su 8:30am-3:45pm. No credit cards. **D12**

FOOD BUDGET

Marcello's
420 Castro St

This no-frills joint serves locally adored pizza with a list of toppings as long as your leg. Slices $2-3; whole pizzas $10-23. Beer $2. Open Su-Th 11am-1am, F-Sa 11am-2am. No credit cards. **C8**

La Méditerranée
2210 Fillmore St

Narrow, colorful, and bustling, La Méditerranée breathes of southern Europe. Lunch specials (about $6.50) and entrees ($7-9) are light and Mediterranean-inspired. Filled phyllo dough ($7.50-9) and quiche of the day ($7) are must-tries. Open Su-Th 11am-10pm, F-Sa 11am-11pm. **C12**

Mela Tandoori
417 O'Farrell St

A clay oven infuses meats with a delicious sweet spiciness. Mood lighting, an indoor fountain, and naan-a-plenty transform chicken tandoori ($9) into an affordable, romantic sample of the Indian subcontinent. Vegetarian options ($6). Open M-Sa 11:30am-2:30pm and 5:30-10:30pm, Su 1-9:30pm. **C14**

Nirvana
544 Castro St

A gorgeous waitstaff, heavenly Thai entrees ($7-12), a plethora of vegetarian options (sauteed, satayed vegetables in Buddha's Garden $11), and drinks like the nirvana colada ($7-8) all help you reach apotheosis in a simple, swanky setting. Open M-Th 4:30-10pm, F 2-10:30pm, Sa 11:30am-10:30pm, Su noon-10pm. **C8**

Pat's Café
2330 Taylor St

One of a string of breakfast joints, Pat's stands out from the crowd, not just because of its bright yellow building, but also for its huge, delicious, home-cooked meals. Burgers, sandwiches, and big breakfasts ($4-7). Open daily 7:30am-2pm. No credit cards. **A14**

Pizza Inferno
1800 Fillmore St

This is one of the trendier pizza parlors around. Lunch specials include a slice of pizza, large salad, and soda ($6). Happy Hour M-F 4-6:30pm and 10-11pm with 2-for-1 pizzas and pitchers of beer for $11. Open daily 11:30am-11pm. **C12**

Stella Pasticceria e Caffé
446 Columbus Av

This family-run establishment serves traditional Italian pastries ($3-6) and coffee ($1.40-2.70). Tip: the sacripantina is their specialty. *Deliziosa!* Open M-W 7:30am-7pm, Th 7:30am-10pm, F-Sa 7:30am-midnight, Su 8:30am-6pm. AmEx/D/MC/V. **B14**

Welcome Home
464 Castro St

If grandma were a drag queen, this would be her kitchen. The crepe paper, antique ovens and pride flags, fried chicken and milkshakes create an all-American and decidedly queer comfort. Dinner $7-10. Open daily 8am-4pm. No credit cards. **C18**

Ananda Fuara   1298 Market St

This vegetarian cafe with vegan tendencies offers creative combinations of super-fresh ingredients—terrific smoothies ($3.25) and great sandwiches like the BBQ tofu burger ($5.75). The house specialty is the "neat-loaf" (with mashed potatoes and gravy, $10.50). A selection of vegan cakes, pies, and cookies ($1-2.50). Open M-Tu and Th-Sa 8am-8pm, W 8am-3pm, occasional Su brunch; call for dates. No credit cards. **D13**

Café Abo   3369 Mission St

A bizarre combination of art gallery, island resort, and political hotspot, Café Abo has some of the best sandwiches ($8-9) and pizzas ($5-6) in the city. Italian-inspired and mostly organic. Open M-F 7:30am-4pm and 6-10pm, Sa 8am-4pm. No credit cards. **D9**

Cafe Venue   721 Market St

Oh, to be a decadent San Franciscan, washing down roasted eggplant on sourdough ($4.50) with a wheatgrass "shot" ($1) to energize for an afternoon of Union Square shopping. The menu offers pasta ($6), smoothies ($3), and spirits. Open M-F 7am-7pm, Sa 8am-5:30pm, Su 11am-5:30pm. No credit cards. **C14**

Charanga   2351 Mission St

Huge portions of tapas ($5.25-13) and some of the tastiest sangria in the Mission. Try the classic, but delicious *maduros*. Wood decor and friendly staff. Open Tu-W 5:30-10pm, Th-Sa 5:30-11pm. MC/V. **C9**

The Golden Turtle   2211 Van Ness Av

Fabulous Vietnamese restaurant serves mind-blowing entrees ($10-15), like the "Look Luck" cubed filet mignon ($12), amid intricately carved walls. Ample options for "the vegetarian gourmet." Open Tu-Su 5-11pm. AmEx/D/MC/V. **B13**

Home   2100 Market ST

Red-hued living room, patio fireplace, and one hot family bring sophistication to this house-warming. Entrees $8-13. Early-bird special includes three-course dinner (Su-Th 5-6pm; $12). "Flip-Flop" cocktail party 2-6pm, dinner 5:30-10pm. Backyard bar open daily 5pm for $5 cocktails. Open M-Th 5:30-10pm, F-Sa 5:30-11pm, and Su brunch 10:30am-3pm ($11). **C9**

Juban   1581 Webster St

Literally "10th" in Japanese, Juban is named after the Yakiniku-style restaurants in the 10th district of Azabu in Tokyo, famous for its hearty meats. Continue the fine tradition of Japanese barbecue—grill meats ($6-8) and vegetables at your table. Enjoy dinner combinations of beef, seafood, and chicken ($17-27), or tasty soup and rice bowls ($6-8). Open M-F 11:30am-2pm and 5-10pm, Sa-Su 11:30am-10pm. AmEx/MC/V. **C12**

Lalitai Thai Restaurant & Bar   96 McAllister St

Mood-lighting, an elaborate water-lily mural, and a touch of plastic foliage give this Thai restaurant an Alice-in-Wonderland, feasting-with-the-frogs feel. Daily and weekly lunch specials $7.25. Most dinner entrees $11, with veggie options. Open M-F 11am-10pm, Sa 11:30am-10pm. **C14**

Lee Hou Restaurant   332 Clement St

Some of the best dim sum New Chinatown has to offer. Service is basic, but come for the food. 13 pieces of dim sum $8. Lunch $4-10. Open Su-Th 8am-1am, F-Sa 8am-2am. **B7**

Pizza Orgasmica   3157 Fillmore St

With pizzas named "menage a trois" and "doggie style," it's hard not to get excited. Prices can get steep (pies $10-23) so don't miss the all-you-can-eat special (11am-4pm; $5.50). Open Su-W 11am-midnight, Th 11am-2:30am, F-Sa 11am-2:30am. **B12**

Ponzu   401 Taylor St

The contemporary Asian cuisine here is popular, tasty, and worth the money. Mongolian lamb ($16) and beef short ribs with green apple ($15) leave no room for veggies but just enough for dessert. Chocolate dim sum for 2 is $12. Feng Shui Happy Hour (M-F 5-7pm) features $3 drinks. Open for breakfast M-F 7-10am, Sa-Su 8-11am; dinner Su-Th 5pm-midnight, F-Sa 5pm-11pm; bar opens at 4:30pm. DJ spins house music Sa 8pm-midnight. AmEx/D/MC/V. **C14**

Squat and Gobble   1428 Haight St

This popular, light-filled cafe offers enormous omelets ($5-7) and equally colossal crepes ($4-7). Lots of salads, sandwiches, and vegetarian options, too. Additional locations: 237 Fillmore St in the Lower Haight and 3600 16th St in the Castro. Open 8am-10pm daily. **D11**

Steps of Rome   348 Columbus Av

Oh-so-suave waiters expertly flirt for tips in this busy, brightly painted cafe. Big menu with lots of vegetarian options. Focaccia sandwiches $5-7; antipasto appetizers $7-10; pasta $7-10; entrees $12-16. Italian beers $4. Sidewalk seating available. 21+ after 6pm. Open M-Th and Su 9am-2am, F-Sa 9am-3am. No credit cards. **B14**

Aperto
1434 18th St

Tagliolini with bacon, jalapeños, and cheese ($11) and made-to-order vegetarian pastas ($10-13) bring Neapolitan summer to this classy but casual setting. Entrees $11-15. Traditional brunch available Sa-Su. Open M-F 11:30am-2:30pm and 5:30-10pm, Sa 11am-2:30pm and 5:30-10pm, Su 10am-2:30pm and 5-9pm. AmEx/MC/V. **C10**

The California Culinary Academy   625 Polk St

This building houses classrooms for 600 culinary students and the affordably upscale Carémé. The kitchen and the dining room are separated by a glass wall so you can watch the chefs work as you enjoy the fruits of their training. Tu-W three-course lunch ($14) and dinners ($24); Th lunch buffet ($20) and French Buffet dinner ($30); F Grande Buffet ($36). Open Tu-F 11:30am-1pm and 6-8pm. AmEx/D/MC/V. **C13**

Equinox   5 Embarcadero Ctr, Hyatt Regency

This extravagant restaurant offers a 360-degree panorama of the city and Bay, while you feast on the finest cuisine. Su champagne brunch ($35) includes omelets, French toast, salads, salmon or chicken entree, and dessert. Daily dinner options range from pasta ($25) to lobster ($39) with a delicious selection of appetizers ($6-12) and desserts ($7-13). Open daily 6-10pm; Su brunch 10am-2pm. AmEx/D/MC/V. **B15**

foreign cinema
2543 Mission St

Foreign cinema takes the dinner and movie narrative to new heights; entertainment is included with each entree. Daily in summer, beginning at dusk, a classic foreign film is projected on a wall in the restaurant. Summer 2003 brought *The Italian Job* and *Crouching Tiger, Hidden Dragon,* among others. From tango and rose endive Caesar salad to Spanish sweet paprika roast chicken and quail, the menu is delectable *and* delicate. They've got a worldly wine list, farmer's market-fresh organic vegetables, and a regular raw oyster bar. Open Tu-Sa 6-10pm, F-Sa 6-11pm, Su 11am-9pm.) **C9**

Greens
Bldg A in Fort Mason

Greens provides Fort Mason citizens with a gourmet dinner eaten while enjoying a view of the water. Vegetables and fish only, cooked into delicious dishes such as Sri Lankan Curry ($18.75), Eggplant Gratin, and Cannellini Bean Soup ($5). Open lunch Tu-Sa noon-2:30pm; Su brunch 10:30am-2pm; dinner M-Sa 5:30-9pm; Greens-to-go M-Th 8am-8pm, F-Sa 8am-5pm, Su 9am-4pm. D/MC/V. **A13**

McCormick and Kuleto's   900 North Point St

Can't leave the wharf without trying crabcakes or clam chowder, but skeptical about the vendors on the piers? This stylish seafood restaurant offers a comprehensive menu and a spectacular view of Aquatic Park. Most entrees $10-25, brick-oven pizzas $7.50-10.50. Open daily 11:30am-11pm. AmEx/D/MC/V. **A13**

Millennium   580 Geary St

In the Savoy Hotel. Millennium's award-winning menu is all vegan, and it was the first restaurant in the US to feature an all-organic wine list. Feast on gourmet cuisine in a romantic, soft-jazz setting. Entrees, like the Szechuan eggplant crêpe, range $13-19 and gather global influences. Reservations recommended. Open daily 5-9pm. **C14**

Pane e Vino   3011 Steiner St

Small, neighborhood trattoria serving classic Italian cuisine. Watch as the chef prepares your pasta ($10-16) or entree ($18-24). Try the *stuffes branzino* (stuffed fish). Open M-Th 11:30am-2:30pm and 5-10pm, F-Sa 11:30am-10:30pm, Su 5-9:30pm. AmEx/MC/V. **B12**

Perry's   1944 Union St

This classic NY-style saloon puts more emphasis on dining than on drinking. Popular with different age groups, but generally frequented by an older, tamer crowd. Customers praise the cheeseburgers (about $10; sandwiches from $9-13; entrees $14-22). Open for breakfast. Kitchen closes 2hr. before bar. Open Su-F 9am-midnight, Sa 9am-1am. AmEx/D/MC/V. **B12**

The Stinking Rose   325 Columbus Av

The world's longest garlic braid hangs in this restaurant, which boasts "We season our garlic with food." "Vampire" (garlic-free) fare available, but what's the point? Appetizers $5-10; pastas $10-15; entrees $14-22; garlic ice cream $4. Open daily 11am-11pm. AmEx/D/MC/V. **B14**

Umeko   1675 Post St

In the Miyako Bldg., upper level. All-you-can-eat Japanese seafood buffet, boasting over 20 kinds of sushi, teriyaki chicken dishes, fresh lobster, and Asian-inspired ice cream. Lunch $12.95 (children under 5 $6.95); dinner $18.95 (children under 5 $9.95). Open Su-Th 11:30am-3:00pm and 5-9:30pm, F-Sa 11:30am-3pm and 5-10pm. AmEx/MC/V. **C13**

Zuni   1658 Market St

Regional French, Italian, and Mediterranean cuisine with a Californian twist and a focus on local organic foods. Heralded as one of the best dining experiences in town. Quite a scene—everyone from the rich and famous to struggling artists. Lunch $9.50-35; dinner $12-35. The $35 roast chicken serves two. Reservations recommended. Open Tu-Sa 11:30am-midnight, Su 11am-11pm. AmEx/MC/V. **D13**

Bambuddha Lounge — 601 Eddy St

Classy chic permeates this South Beach-style lounge. Lots of outdoor seating, enormous bed-like couches, and nightly DJs (house on weekends, more mellow mood music during the week) make this one of San Francisco's newest hotspots. A definite must-see, even if the drinks are a little pricier than most other bars in the area (cocktails $6-9). AmEx/MC/V. **C13**

The Bigfoot Lodge — 1750 Polk St

Campy bear heads, a gigantic Big Foot, and bartenders uniformed as scouts keep up more of an image than does the easy-going crowd in this log cabin retreat. Beer $3.50-4.50, cocktails around $5. Happy Hour daily from opening until 8pm. Open M-F 3pm-2am, Sa-Su noon-2am. **B13**

Blind Tiger — 787 Broadway

Named after the Prohibition custom of displaying a stuffed tiger to identify an establishment as a speakeasy, Blind Tiger is outfitted in a high Mandarin style. This upscale lounge and dance floor lives up to the implied Chinese-American fusion as a young crowd sips specialty cocktails ($5-6) and visits the sake bar amid Chinese wall hangings. Resident DJs spin house and R&B. 21+. Cover varies after 10pm. Open Th-Sa 8pm-2am. MC/V. **B14**

Edinburgh Castle — 950 Geary St

Lads and lassies drink Tennant's and Guinness and eat fish and chips at this watering hole. Non-image-conscious crowd unwinds with $4 beer and occasionally with local bands F-Sa. Lots of interesting literary-themed parties like Big Brother Night and readings by young, new writers. Cover only on nights with events. Happy Hour 5-7pm. Open daily 5pm-2am. MC/V. **C13**

Hotel Utah Saloon — 500 4th St

Excellent and unpretentious saloon—with an original Belgian Bar from 1908—and one of the friendliest crowds around. More than your average bar food, including build your own burgers (from $7). Downstairs stage hosts live rock or country music nightly and one of the best open mics in the city on M (shows begin 8:30-9pm). Beer $3.75. 21+. Show cover $3-7. Open M-F 11:30am-2am, Sa-Su 6pm-2am. **D15**

Hush Hush — 496 14th St

You'll feel oh so hip when you find Hush Hush, since this hot spot is too cool to need a sign; look for the blue awning with 496 in white. Large leather booths, pool, and local DJs spinning almost every night have everyone whispering about this place. MC Battle 1st Tu of every month. Smile Su with Rock DJs. Open daily 6pm-2am. No credit cards. **C9**

The Irish Bank   10 Mark La

An authentic Irish bar, with an award-winning scotch list, super pub-grub and a friendly staff that creates a homey atmosphere. Caters to a mixed crowd of tourists, unwinding suits, and ex-pats. Visit on Sunday to share a cracking ploughman's lunch ($7) and a pint ($3-4) with people from the old-country. Open daily 11:30am-1:30am. AmEx/MC/V. **C14**

Lefty O'Doul's   333 Geary St

Named after iconic baseball hero Frank "Lefty" O'Doul, this colossal Irish tavern is three smaller bars in one: a piano lounge, a vast bar and buffet with booths and sit-down tables, and a sports bar in the back. Most drinks are $4. Nightly piano sing-along. Open daily 7am-2am; kitchen closes at midnight. MC/V. **C14**

The Lost & Found Saloon   1353 Grant Av

A shabby blue velvet and wood bar whose past lives include Miss Smith's Tea Room, where the Beats flocked for poetry and bebop, and the Coffee Gallery, where a young Janis Joplin got her start. Performances nightly. Cover $5. Open daily noon-2am. No credit cards. **B14**

Lush Lounge   1092 Post St

Some of the best bartenders in the city shake their cocktails for an upscale but eclectic crowd. $4 speciality drinks, a steady stream of ABBA and Madonna, and the best chocolate martinis in the city. Happy Hour 4-9pm. Open M-Tu 5pm-2am, W-Su 4pm-2am. No credit cards. **C13**

Noc Noc   557 Haight St

Cavernous, colorful chaos, padded floor seating, and a DJ spinning hip-hop, jazz, and rock. Micros, imports, bottled Belgians, and some *sake*. Happy Hour daily until 7pm, all pints $2.50. Magic Hour Tarot Readings M 7-10pm. Open daily 5pm-2am. MC/V. **D12**

Place Pigalle   520 Hayes St

After a long day at work, the designers and artists of Hayes St relax on vintage velvet sofas at this big, dark, airy bar. Weekend nights the wine flows freely, the music blares, and crowds of 20-somethings with bohemian sensibilities pack the place. Occasional DJs and a rotating art exhibit. Happy Hour daily 4-7pm (beer $2.75). Open daily 4pm-2am. **D13**

Wish Lounge   1539 Folsom St

Plush leather couches and deep red lighting make this new SoMa hotspot a must for the young and hip. But underneath the uber-cool decor, the laid-back crowd, the good drinks (cocktails $4-5, beer $4), and the very hot and fast bartenders help Wish achieve that delicate balance between chic and actually fun. Open M-F 5pm-2am, Sa 7pm-2am. AmEx/MC/V. **D14**

BARS & PUBS NIGHTLIFE

111 Minna
111 Minna St

"Art and Leisure" at this funky up-and-comer's gallery by day, hipster groove-spot by night. Cocktails and beer $3-10. Open M-Tu noon-10pm, W noon-11pm, Th-F noon-2am, Sa 10pm-2am, Su 9pm-2am. Cover $5-15 for bands and progressive house DJs. **C15**

Club Six
60 6th St

A large, comfy upstairs for chilling and a more raging downstairs for flailing limbs. The schedule and DJs change every weekend but Club Six is known for its consistently good music in six different dance areas, late hours, and young crowds. Great place to hang out or groove on weekends. Beer $5, cocktails $6. Cover $5-10. Open Th 9pm-2am, F-Sa 9pm-4am. No credit cards. **C14**

Diva's
1081 Post St

Billed as San Francisco's only full-time transgender nightclub, the layout is as diverse as the clientele (men, women, and everyone between and around flock to Diva's on weekends). Take in the the three floors of dancing, pool tables, and plush couches, or sit back and enjoy a good, old-fashioned drag show (F-Sa 12:30am). Cover $10, ladies free before 11pm. Happy Hour M-F 5-7pm. Open daily 6am-2am. No credit cards. **C13**

Liquid
2925 16th St

Nightly mix usually includes trip-hop and hip-hop, but mainly house. Young but mellow crowd fills the small space. Meet a cutie and practice those long-forgotten back seat skills; all of Liquid's couches are car seats. 21+. Cover $4-5. Open daily 9pm-3am. No credit cards. **C9**

Nickie's BBQ
460 Haight St

After many incarnations (including a brothel where Nickie worked), this venue has evolved into one of the chillest, friendliest clubs in the city. Live DJ M-Sa. Grateful Dead M, world music T, reggae W, and an eclectic mix of funk, hip-hop, and dance music. Cover $5. Open daily 9pm-2am. No credit cards. **D12**

Odeon Bar
3223 Mission St

Fun and quirky artists' hangout in the deep Mission. Offbeat and off the beaten path. Nightly events, like Card Trick Sa. Inquire here about the Burning Man festival; this is one of its SF hubs. Open daily 4pm-2am. Accepts "every credit card that's neither expired nor stolen." **B9**

Polly Esther's
181 Eddy St

Savor the anachronism of this touristy retro dig where Le Freak plays as you sip "Brady Punch" cock-tails ($7) under a velvet Top Gun painting. Downstairs **Culture Club** spins 80s. Cover F $10, Sa $12-15. No cover Th or before 9pm. Open Th 9pm-3am, F-Sa 8pm-4am. MC/V. **DC4**

El Rio   3158 Mission St

A classy, mixed club with stylish lighting and decor, large outdoor patio, and well-groomed bartenders. Salsa Su, including a dance lesson and patio barbecue. F 5-7pm free oysters on the half-shell. Drinks $4-10. Occasional cover $5-8. Open M-Th 5pm-2am, F-Su 3pm-2am. No credit cards. **D9**

Royale   1326 Grant Av

A small, dimly lit, deep blue club that's got local R&B DJs spinning Tu-Sa. Mainstream on weekends, more underground during the week. Packed to the brim on F and Sa night; the door often closes at 11pm. Happy Hour 7-9pm with specials on beer and drinks ($3). Cover $3-5 after 10pm. Su nights Royale turns into a much more mellow neighborhood bar. Open Su-W 7pm-2am, Th-Sa 5pm-2am. AmEx/MC/V. **B14**

Ruby Skye   420 Mason St

Explore your rhythm at the restored 1896 Stage Door Theater (stained-glass windows intact) with a million other downtown clubbers and a million-and-one out-of-town partiers. You may look inadequate compared to the jaw-dropping go-go dancers, but so will everyone else despite the dress code ("fashionable attire" required, no jeans F-Sa). Dependable house DJs. Drinks from $5. Cover W-Th $10, F-Sa $20. 21+. Open W-Sa 7pm-3am. AmEx/D/MC/V. **C14**

The Top   424 Haight St

Host to some of the finest house DJs in SF. A definite must for turntable loyalists. Su House and M Hip Hop are huge. House on W and F, too. Drum and Bass Tu and Sa. Happy Hour until 10pm. 21+. Cover $5 after 10pm. Open daily 7pm-2am. No credit cards. **D12**

Velvet Lounge   443 Broadway

Decked-out 20- and 30-somethings pack this club and thump along to top 40, hip-hop, and house. F occasional live cover bands. No sneakers or athletic wear. Cover usually $10. Open W-Sa 9pm-2am. **B14**

Up and Down Club   1151 Folsom St

At this two-level club, the downstairs is an international fusion restaurant during the day and dance hotspot at night, while the upstairs feels more like a bar. DJs on the two floors spin hip-hop, house, and funk. On W Hump Night, no cover and $3 drinks help you over hump day. Open M-F 11am-3pm for lunch and low-key mingling and Tu-Su 9pm-2am for drinks and dancing. Cover F-Sa $5-8. D/MC/V. **D14**

CLUBS NIGHTLIFE

The Bar on Castro   456 Castro St

A refreshingly urbane Castro staple with dark plush couches perfect for eyeing the stylish young crowd, scoping the techno-raging dance floor, or watching Queer as Folk on Su. Happy Hour M-F 3-8pm (beer $2.25). Su beer $1.75. Open M-F 4pm-2am, Sa-Su noon-2am. No credit cards. **C8**

The Café   2367 Market St

The Café is chill in the afternoon with pool and pinball, but come evening, it morphs into speaker-pumping house- and pop-remix bliss. Repeat *Guardian* awards for best gay bar. No cover. Open M-F 2pm-2am, Sa-Su 12:30pm-2am. No credit cards. **C8**

The EndUp   401 6th St

A San Francisco institution where everyone eventually ends up. DJs spin progressive house for the mostly straight KitKat Th, the pretty-boy Fag F, and the hetero-homo mix during popular all-day Sa-Su parties. Sa morning "Otherwhirled" party 4am. Infamous Su 'T' Dance 6pm-4am. Cover $5-15. Open Th 10:30pm-4 am, F 10pm-4am, Sa 6am-noon and 10pm-4am and Su 6am-4am. No credit cards. **D14**

Esta Noche   3079 16th St

Where the Mission meets the Castro. The city's premier gay Latino bar hosts regular drag shows. The bar is quite popular and space is tight on weekends. Domestic bottles and drafts $2.25. Happy Hour daily 4-9pm. Cover F-Su $5-10. Open Su-Th 1pm-2am, F-Sa 1pm-2am. No credit cards. **C9**

The Lexington Club   3464 19th St

The only bar in San Francisco that is all lesbian, all the time. Jukebox plays all the grrly favorites. Though there's not much room for dancing, bar-goers sometimes spill out into the streets. Tarot Tu with Jessica. Happy Hour M-F 3-7pm. Open daily 3pm-2am. No credit cards. **C9**

The Stud   399 9th St

This legendary bar and club recreates itself every night of the week—go Tu for the wild and wacky midnight drag and transgender shows, Th for Reform School boy-cruising party, F for ladies' night, Sa for Sugar's free delicious eye-candy. Crowd is mostly gay. Cover $5-9. Open M, W, F, and Su 5pm-2am, Tu 5pm-3am, Th and Sa 5pm-4am. No credit cards. **D14**

Wild Side West   424 Cortland Av

The oldest lesbian bar in SF is a neighborhood favorite for women and men alike. There's pool, a cool jukebox, cheap beer ($2.50-3.50), and a friendly atmosphere. The hidden highlight is a junkyard jungle with benches, fountains, and scrap-art statues in back. Open daily 1pm-2am. No credit cards. **D9**

NIGHTLIFE GAY & LESBIAN

Café Macondo — 3159 16th St

Macondo is all that a coffeehouse should be. Mismatched comfy old furniture to sink into and shelves of books for those who forgot their own. Sandwiches $4.25-5; salads $3.75-6; dinner entrees $5-6.50. Coffee and drinks $1.25-2.75. Open M-F 10am-10pm, Sa 11am-10pm. No credit cards. **C9**

Café du Nord — 2170 Market St

Takes you back in time to a red velvet club with speakeasy ambience. Excellent live music nightly—from pop and groove to garage rock. Favorites include vintage jazz, blues, and R&B. Special weekly events include the popular Monday Night Hoot, a showcase of local singing and songwriting talent. Dinner served 5:30-11pm. Happy Hour 6-7:30pm with swank $2.50 martinis, Manhattans, and cosmos. 21+. Cover $5-10 after 8:30pm. Open daily 6pm-2am. No credit cards. **C8**

Caffè Trieste — 601 Vallejo St

Though every bar in North Beach claims to be a Beat haunt, this is the genuine article. While Vesuvio's is where the gang got trashed, Trieste remained their more mellow living room. The leftovers still hang out in the front. It hasn't changed much since then—a few new photos of famous patrons, but the jukebox still plays opera, and it's still the cornerstone of North Beach's remaining Italian community. Live Italian pop and opera concerts every Sa 1:45-6pm (since 1973) alone are worth a stop here. Espresso drinks $1.50-3.25; bottles of beer $2-3; glasses of wine $2.25-3.75. Open M-Sa 10am-6pm. No credit cards. **B14**

The Horseshoe Café — 566 Haight St

Big-screen TV, movie, and music video projections in the back. DSL Internet access and plenty of space to read, write, or ruminate over chai iced tea ($2.25), coffee ($1.25), or cookies (50¢). Open daily 6am-midnight. No credit cards. **D12**

Spike's — 4117 19th St

Candy, sweets, and dog-friendly treats at this juice and coffee joint merit walking with Fido away from the center of Castro Village. Neighborly Spike's place is also one of the few cafes with seating. Open daily 6:30am-8pm. **C8**

Vesuvio Café — 255 Columbus Av

Jack and his friends started their day by howling like Dharma Bums over pints at Vesuvio and then café-crawled their way up Columbus Av. The wooden, tiled, and stained-glass bar with an upstairs balcony remains a great place to drink. Draught beers $4.25, bottled beers $3.50, pitchers $9-12. Happy Hour M-Th 3-7pm: drinks $1 off, pitchers and bottles of wine $3 off. Open daily 6am-2am. No credit cards. **B14**

COFFEEHOUSES NIGHTLIFE

CLASSICAL & OPERA

San Francisco Opera
301 Van Ness Av

Open for tickets 2hr. before shows. Box office, 199 Grove St. Open M-Sa 10am-6pm. Tickets from $23. Standing-room tickets ($10 cash) from 10am. **D13**

San Francisco Symphony
201 Van Ness Av

The acoustics here are slightly off, but you get an excellent head-on view of the conductor from the cheapest seats. Prices vary. Open M-F 9am-5pm. **D13**

ROCK & BLUES

Bimbo's 365 Club
1025 Columbus Av

Keeping the party going since 1931. Bimbo's now hosts prestigious acts from swing to indie rock. Two-drink minimum. Tickets around $15. Box office open M-F 10am-4pm. MC/V. **A14**

Bottom of the Hill
1233 17th St

Three bands—some local, some bigger names—nightly. Su afternoon all-you-can-eat barbecues (most Su, $5-10). Happy Hour F 3pm-7pm, $1 beers. 21+. Cover most nights, $5-12. Open M-Th 8:30pm-2am, F 3pm-2am, Sa 8:30pm-2am, Su hours vary. MC/V. **C10**

The Fillmore
1805 Geary Blvd

In Japantown. The legendary foundation of San Francisco's music and cultural scene. Tickets $15-40. Call for hours. Wheelchair-accessible. AmEx/MC/V. **C12**

Slim's
333 11th St

Slim's low-key bar, food, and dedication to blues, R&B, jazz, Cajun, and alternative make this venue a favorite. All ages. Tickets $10-25. Box office open M-F 10:30am-6pm. MC/V. **D14**

HIP-HOP & JAZZ

Justice League
628 Divisadero St

Live hip-hop is hard to find, but the Justice League fights for a good beat. M 10pm Club Dred, reggae and dub. W 10pm Bang Bang, soul night. 21+. Cover $5-25. Usually open daily 9pm-2am. **D12**

Jazz at Pearl's
256 Columbus Av

Traditional jazz for a casual crowd. Light menu $4-9. 21+. No cover, 2-drink min. Open M-Sa 8:30pm-2am. **B14**

THEATER

Club Fugazi
678 Green St

Catch cabaret-style *Beach Blanket Babylon*, a long-running and always entertaining San Francisco classic, here. Now in its 30th year! Tickets $25-70. 21+ except

Su 3pm. Shows W-Th 8pm, F-Sa 7 and 10pm, Su 3 and 7pm. Box office open M-Sa 10am-6pm, Su noon-6pm. MC/V. **B14**

Magic Theatre   Fort Mason Ctr, Bldg D

Sam Shepard served as playwright-in-residence at the Magic Theatre from 1975 to 1985. Today, the theater stages exclusively premiere shows. W-Th $22-32, F-Su $27-37. Senior and student rush tickets (available 30min. before the show, $10). Shows start at 8 or 8:30pm. Su matinees 2:30pm ($15), reduced cost for previews ($17). Box office open Tu-Sa noon-5pm. AmEx/D/MC/V. **A13**

The Orpheum   1192 Market St

Box Office is on 6th St at Market St. This famous San Francisco landmark hosts the big Broadway shows. BART entrance in front of theater. Past shows include *Phantom of the Opera, Chicago,* and *The Graduate.* Wheelchair-accessible. Two sister theaters in the area host smaller shows: Golden Gate Theatre, 1 Taylor St, and Curran Theatre, 445 Geary St. AmEx/D/MC/V. **A13**

DANCE

Alonzo King's Lines Contemporary Ballet

Dancers combine classical moves with athletic flair to great jazz and world music. Springtime shows at the Yerba Buena Center for the Arts. Tickets $15-25. **C14**

Dancer's Group   3252A 19th St

Near Shotwell St, in the Mission. Promotes cultural dance and original works. Open M-F 10am-4pm. **C10**

Oberlin Dance Company   3153 17th St

Mainly dance, but occasional theater space with gallery attached. 2-6 shows a week. Tickets $10-20, but occasional 2-for-1 and "pay what you can" nights. Box office open W-Sa 2-5pm. AmEx/MC/V. **C9**

San Francisco Ballet   301 Van Ness Av

Shares the War Memorial Opera House with the San Francisco Opera. Tickets from $30. Discounted standing-room-only tickets are available at the Opera House 2hr. before performances. **D13**

SAN FRANCISCO SPORTS TEAMS

Football: San Francisco 49ers, at 3COM Park. Tickets ☎ 656-4900. Formerly known as Candlestick Park, home to the San Francisco Giants. As close to the ocean as a stadium can be.

Baseball: San Francisco Giants, at Pacific Bell Park in SoMa. Tickets 888-464-2468.

DANCE & SPORTS ENTERTAINMENT

FESTIVALS & EVENTS

January-February: San Francisco Independent Film Festival.

January 19-21: Dr. Martin Luther King Jr.'s Birthday Celebration, in Yerba Buena Gardens.

Late February: Chinese New Year Celebration and Parade. Parade starts at Market and 2nd St. around 5:30pm.

March 10-14: International Asian-American Film Festival.

March 18: St. Patrick's Day Parade.

April 23: Cherry Blossom Festival, Japantown.

April-May: San Francisco International Film Festival, at the Kabuki and Castro Theaters.

Early May: A Fair to Remember, in Golden Gate Park.

June 26-27: San Francisco International Gay and Lesbian Film Festival, at the Roxie and Castro Theatres.

June-August: Stern Grove San Francisco Midsummer Music Festival, in Stern Grove, south of Golden Gate Park. Free performances Su 2pm.

June 11-13: San Francisco Black Film Festival.

June 27: Pride Day. Parade and events start at 10:30am.

Late July: San Francisco Jewish Film Festival.

July 15: Cable Car Bell-Ringing Championship, Fisherman's Wharf or Union Sq.

Late July: North Beach Jazz Festival.

Early August: Nihonmachi Street Fair in Japantown. Lion dancers, *taiko* drummers, and karaoke wars.

September: San Francisco Shakespeare Festival, in Golden Gate Park. Free.

September 9: San Francisco Fringe Festival, at several theaters downtown.

Early September: Ghirardelli Square Chocolate Festival.

Mid-September: Vivas Las Americas! at Pier 39. Music and dance celebrate Hispanic heritage.

Late September: San Francisco Blues Festival, in Fort Mason.

Late September: Chinatown Autumn Moon Festival, on Grant Av, with martial arts and lion dancing.

September 26: Folsom Street Fair, on the last Su in Sept. Pride Day's ruder, raunchier, rowdier brother.

October 30-31: Great Pumpkin Weigh-Off, followed by Halloween San Francisco.

October 2: Castro Street Fair. Food, live music, and art.

November 13: Italian Heritage Parade and Festival, in North Beach.

November 15: San Francisco Jazz Festival.

November 23-December 24: Fantasy of Lights. Sunset Light parade complements illuminated buildings in Union Sq.

December 10-17: Festival of Lights, at Union Sq. Festivities lead up to the lighting of a huge menorah.

ENTERTAINMENT FESTIVALS & EVENTS

BOOKS & MUSIC

Amoeba Music   1855 Haight St
Rolling Stone dubbed this the best record store in the world. The Haight St. Amoeba stocks an amazing selection of used CDs, plus new music and a parade of vintage concert posters. Open M-Sa 10:30am-10pm, Su 11am-9pm. D/MC/V. **C8**

City Lights Bookstore   261 Columbus Av
In North Beach. A Beat generation landmark. Open daily 10am-midnight. **B14**

A Different Light Bookstore   489 Castro St
In the Castro. All queer, all the time. The ultimate resource for free Bay Area mags and host to a popular community bulletin board. Open daily 10am-10pm. **C8**

Recycled Records   1377 Haight St
RR fights the good fight for the preservation of analog sound. Vinyl is king, but CDs and some DVDs are infiltrating the vast collection ($3-15). Open M-F 10am-8pm, Sa 10am-9pm, Su 11am-7pm. AmEx/MC/V. **D11**

CLOTHES & VINTAGE

Bulo   418 Hayes St
Stylish and unusual collections of shoes. Expensive ($99-450), but look for great sales. Men's shoes across the street at 437-A Hayes St. Open M-Sa 11am-7pm, Su noon-6pm. AmEx/D/MC/V. **D13**

M   1425 Grant St
A small store crammed with vintage clothes of the female variety, mostly $25-40 per piece. Homemade beanies and crochet hats $20-45. Open daily from 9:30am. AmEx/MC/V. **B14**

Manifesto   514 Octavia St
Local designer makes 1950s-inspired clothes for men and women. The retro-looking dresses and shirts are well cut, reasonably priced ($65-150), and more flattering than many of their authentic cousins. Open Tu-F 11am-7pm, Sa 11am-6pm, Su noon-5pm. AmEx/MC/V. **D13**

SPECIALTY STORES

House of Magic   2025 Chestnut St
A colorful jungle of magic tricks, gags, wigs, and lowbrow laughs. Open M-Sa 10am-7pm, Su 11am-4pm. AmEx/D/MC/V. **A12**

Under One Roof   549 Castro St
More sophisticated than your average kitsch shop, Under One Roof donates 100% of the profit from every sale to organizations working to fight AIDS. Open M-Sa 10am-8pm, Su 11am-7pm. AmEx/D/MC/V. **C8**

SAN FRANCISCO MUNICIPAL RAILWAY (MUNI)

This system of buses, cable cars, subways, and streetcars is the most efficient way to get around the city. Runs daily 6am-1am. $1.25, seniors and ages 5-17 $0.35. **MUNI passports** are valid on all MUNI vehicles (1-day $9, 3-day $15, 7-day $20). Weekly Pass ($9) is valid for a single work week and requires an additional $1 to ride the cable cars. **Owl Service** runs limited routes daily 1-5am. Wheelchair access varies among routes; all below-ground stations, but not all above-ground sites, are accessible. (☎673-6864; www.sfmuni.com.)

CABLE CARS

Noisy, slow, and usually crammed full, but charming relics. To avoid mobs, ride in the early morning. The **Powell-Mason (PM)** line, which runs to the wharf, is the most popular. The **California (C)** line, from the Financial District up through Nob Hill, is usually the least crowded, but the **Powell-Hyde (PH)** line, with the steepest hills and the sharpest turns, may be the most fun. $3, seniors and disabled $2, under 6 free; before 7am and after 9pm $1. No transfers.

BAY AREA RAPID TRANSIT (BART)

Operates trains along 4 lines connecting San Francisco with the **East Bay,** including Oakland, Berkeley, Concord, and Fremont. All stations provide maps and schedules. There are 8 BART stops in San Francisco proper, but BART is not a local transportation system. Runs M-F 4am-midnight, Sa 6am-midnight, Su 8am-midnight. $1.15-4.90. Wheelchair-accessible. (☎989-2278; www.bart.org.)

CAR RENTAL

City   ☎877-861-1312
1748 Folsom St. Compacts from $29-35 per day, $160-170 per week. 21+; under 25 $8 per day surcharge. **D13**

Thrifty   ☎415-788-8111
520 Mason St. Compacts from $27 per day. Unlimited mileage. 21+; under 25 $25 per day surcharge. **C14**

TAXIS

City Wide Dispatch	☎415-920-0715
Luxor Cab	☎415-282-4141
National Cab Company	☎415-648-4444
Town Taxi	☎415-285-3800
Yellow Cab	☎415-626-2345

TRANSPORTATION

EMERGENCY

Emergency	☎ 911
Fire	☎ 415-558-3200
Police	☎ 415-553-0123
Poison	☎ 800-876-4766

CRISIS & HELP LINES

AIDS Hotline	☎ 800-342-2437
Disabilities Crisis Line	☎ 800-426-4263
Drug Crisis Line	☎ 415-362-3400
Rape Crisis Center	☎ 415-647-7273
Suicide Prevention	☎ 415-781-0500
Youth Crisis Hotline	☎ 800-448-4663

BICYCLE AND SKATE RENTAL

Blazing Saddles ☎ 415-202-8888

1095 Columbus Av, at Francisco St. Bikes $7 per hr., $28 per day; kids' bikes $20 per day. Open daily 8am-8pm. AmEx/MC/V. **A14**

Skates on Haight ☎ 415-752-8375

1818 Haight St. In-line skates $6 per hr., $24 per day; scooters $7/$28. Open M-F 11am-7pm, Sa-Su 10am-6pm. AmEx/D/MC/V. **C8**

HOSPITALS

Central Public Health Center ☎ 415-271-4263

470 27th St, at Telegraph Av in Oakland. Make appointments in advance. Open M-F 8-11:30am and 1-4pm.

Haight-Ashbury Free Clinic ☎ 415-487-5632

558 Clayton St, at Haight St. Appointments only. Open M-Th 9am-9pm, F 1-5pm. **D11**

LAUNDROMATS

Doo Wash ☎ 415-885-1222

817 Columbus Av, near Lombard St in **North Beach.** Video games, pinball machines, pool table, and TV. Wash $1.50; dry $1. Open daily 7am-11pm, last load 9:30pm. **A14**

Self-Service Laundromat

600 Bush St, near Stockton St in **Union Sq.** Wash $1.75; dry 25¢ per 10min. Open daily 7am-10pm, last load 9pm. **B14**

FINANCIAL SERVICES

American Express ☎ 415-536-2600

455 Market St. Open M-F 9am-5:30pm, Sa 10am-2pm. Additional locations: 311 9th Av (☎ 415-221-6760), 1585 Sloat Blvd (☎ 415-242-0277). **B15**

STREET INDEX

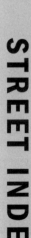

STREET INDEX

SIGHT INDEX

SIGHT INDEX